The Inuit

ERINN BANTING

Weigl

CALGARY

www.weigl.com

Published by Weigl Educational Publishers Limited
6325 10 Street SE
Calgary, Alberta, Canada
T2H 2Z9

Website: www.weigl.com

Library and Archives Canada Cataloguing in Publication Data

Banting, Erinn, 1976-
    The Inuit / Erinn Banting.

(Canadian Aboriginal art and culture)
Includes index.
ISBN 978-1-55388-325-8 (bound)
ISBN 978-1-55388-326-5 (pbk.)

    1. Inuit--Canada--Juvenile literature. I. Title. II. Series.
E99.E7B355 2007   j971.9004'9712   C2007-902183-2

Printed in Canada
1 2 3 4 5 6 7 8 9 0 11 10 09 08 07

Project Coordinator Heather Kissock   **Design** Janine Vangool

Photograph credits
Every reasonable effort has been made to trace ownership and to obtain permission to reprint copyright material. The publishers would be pleased th have any errors or omissions brought to their attention so that they may be corrected in subsequent printings.

Cover (top right): courtesy of the City of Iqaluit; © **Canadian Museum of Civilization:** pages 11 (IV-C-5142, S95-24811), 15 top (IV-C-3498 a-b, D2003-17336), and 15 bottom (IX-C:2846, S95-32575); **Courtesy of the City of Iqaluit:** pages 3, 6, 10, 12, 17, 25, 28, and 30; **Glenbow Archives:** page 18 (nd-1-3).

We acknowledge the financial support of the Government of Canada through the Book Publishing Industry Development Program (BPIDP) for our publishing activities.

Please note
All of the Internet URLs given in the book were valid at the time of publication. However, due to the dynamic nature of the Internet, some addresses may have changed, or sites may have ceased to exist since publication. While the author and publisher regret any inconvenience this may cause readers, no responsibility for any such changes can be accepted by either the author or the publisher.

CONTENTS

The People

Nearly 1,000 years ago, Inuit **ancestors** called the Thule arrived in Canada's Far North. They travelled hundreds of miles from Alaska and settled in the parts of Canada now known as Nunavut, the Northwest Territories, and northern Quebec.

The Inuit became a large group that was spread across northern North America. Many Inuit moved from one place to another during different seasons. Inuit life was based on the **migration** cycles of various animal herds, including the caribou. As these animals were an important food source, the Inuit followed the herds wherever they went.

Inuit Map

This map shows the traditional lands of the Inuit in Canada.

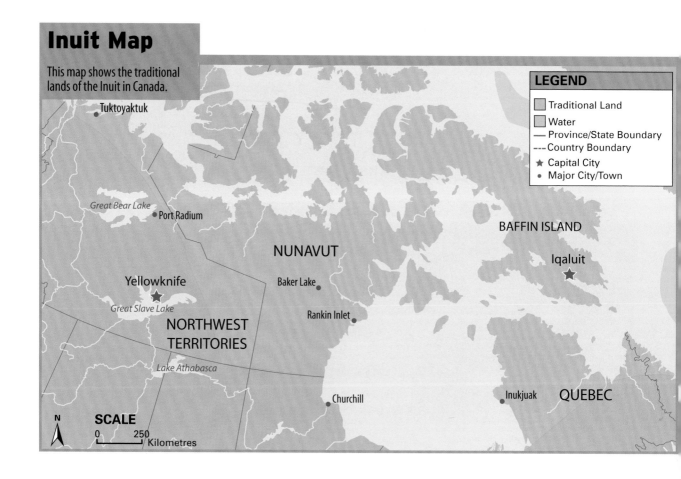

LEGEND
- Traditional Land
- Water
- — Province/State Boundary
- --- Country Boundary
- ★ Capital City
- • Major City/Town

Tuktoyaktuk

Great Bear Lake
• Port Radium

BAFFIN ISLAND

NUNAVUT

Iqaluit ★

Yellowknife ★
Baker Lake •

Great Slave Lake

Rankin Inlet •

NORTHWEST
TERRITORIES

Lake Athabasca

Churchill •

Inukjuak • QUEBEC

N

SCALE
0   250
Kilometres

Inuit homes were based on the needs of the season. In summer, the Inuit lived in tents made from wood and animal skins. In the winter, they lived in houses made from sod, stone, or ice and snow. In some parts of Canada, the Inuit lived in igloos. These are houses made from blocks of ice.

MODERN LIVING

Today, most Inuit live in cities across Canada, or in settlements in Nunavut, the Northwest Territories, and northern Quebec. Few rely on hunting for survival. Life for the Inuit today is similar to those of Canadians across the country. Many communities are working to develop new **economic** opportunities within their area. They are also working hard to preserve their language and **traditions**.

Caribou can travel more than 4,800 kilometres in a single year. They travel farther than any other land animal.

Inuit Homes

The Arctic is one of the most difficult places to live on Earth. Wild winds, cold temperatures, ice, and snowy conditions made shelter very important to its early inhabitants. The Inuit lived in different types of homes at different times of year.

In the summer, the Inuit built tents made from sturdy frames covered in animal skins. The frames were made from wood poles or the giant rib bones of whales. The poles were spread out in a circle. One end of the poles was fastened into the ground in a circle. The other end was tied together to form a triangular structure. The skins of caribou or other animals were fastened around the frame.

In the winter, most Inuit lived in igloos, but some lived in permanent homes. These were usually made from stone and were oval-shaped. The foundation was built into the ground so the homes would not shift or collapse when the ground thawed and froze each year.

When building an igloo, one person works from the inside. This way, he or she can adjust the blocks of snow and fill the cracks that form between them.

WINTER DWELLING

Hundreds of years ago, some of the Inuit inhabiting Canada's Arctic region lived in igloos during the cold winter months. To build these icy dwellings, the Inuit carved large blocks of ice from the frozen landscape. These blocks were stacked in a circle, and the cracks between them were filled with loose snow.

Igloos are sturdy shelters. They can provide protection against very strong winds.

Each layer of the igloo was made with smaller blocks so that they eventually formed a dome at the top. The entranceway to the igloo was just big enough for a person to crawl through. Inside, the doorway was blocked with animal skins so that heat could not escape and cold air could not blow in.

Often, groups of igloos were built together to form villages. People would leave to hunt during the day and return to their villages in the evening. Even larger groups of igloos were sometimes used for special celebrations. These igloos were connected by tunnels and could hold up to 20 people.

Inuit Communities

Life in the frozen Arctic is challenging. Icy conditions mean few plants can survive. The people living there cannot rely on farming for food. The Inuit have a long tradition of working together to hunt, fish, build communities, and survive.

In the winter, several families lived and worked together. Men fished and hunted animals such as caribou, whales, and seals. Although some women joined hunting expeditions, most stayed home and cared for the children, prepared food, and made clothing.

Hunters sometimes stand for hours waiting for seals to come up to their breathing holes.

Iqaluit is the capital of Nunavut. The name Iqaluit means "place of many fish."

The Inuit governed their communities using the principles of cooperation. They shared the land and looked to the **elders** to lead their settlements. Elders advised when to fish, hunt, harvest, and go to war.

Most Inuit continued to live a traditional lifestyle, relying on hunting and fishing for food, clothing, and trade, until the mid-1900s. Then, European influences began to have an impact on their lives. Advances in transportation, housing, and industry have all become part of Inuit life.

The arrival of Europeans created many challenges for the Inuit. European settlers claimed and developed parts of the North. As a result, the Inuit lost control of their traditional hunting grounds. Communities throughout the region have fought to regain their lands and the right to govern themselves. In 1999, the Canadian government divided the Northwest Territories and created a new **territory** called Nunavut. As part of Nunavut's formation, the Canadian government granted the Inuit control of 351,000 square kilometres of the new territory. The Inuit were also given hunting and fishing rights, mining rights for certain areas, and a payment of $1.17 billion to help develop the territory. The Canadian government remains active in Nunavut. It works closely with members of the Inuit community to ensure that Inuit concerns and traditions are addressed through the territory's own system of government.

Inuit Clothing

Early Inuit inhabitants made clothing from the furs and skins of animals they hunted for food. The animal hides kept them warm in the harsh Arctic **climate**. Caribou and seal were used most often, but other animals were used as well.

Thick pants and large parkas made from caribou protected people from freezing wind, ice, and snow. Parkas worn by men and women were slightly different. Men's parkas had smaller hoods to make sure they could see while they were hunting. Women's parkas had a special pouch to hold young children.

Traditional Inuit clothing is an expression of the Inuit culture.

The Inuit also wore thick mittens and *kamiks*, or boots. Sealskin was used to make mittens because it was water resistant and strong. Kamiks could be made from either caribou or seal. If the boots were to be used on land only, they were made from caribou skin. If they were to be used in water, sealskin was used. In very cold times of year, people sometimes would wear up to four layers of protection on their feet.

Many Inuit people made beautifully decorated clothing for special occasions or dances. Prior to the arrival of Europeans, these decorations included products made from the natural environment, such as fringes made from rabbit fur. When Europeans arrived, they traded with the Inuit. In exchange for animal hides, they gave the Inuit beads, metal, and fabric. These items were used to decorate traditional clothing.

Today, Inuit people celebrate their **heritage** by wearing traditional clothing at special ceremonies and events. Many craftspeople have learned how to make the special clothing and have passed that art down to the generations that follow them.

Europeans introduced beads, thread, wool, fabrics, and needles made from metal instead of bone to the Inuit. These materials changed the way the Inuit made clothing. Beads were sewn into their clothing in geometric shapes or patterns as decoration. Fabric was also used to decorate clothing. The Mother Hubbard is a style of parka designed by the Inuit. The coats have a fabric shell that is decorated with embroidered patterns.

Inuit Food

Finding food in the Arctic can be challenging. With very limited resources, the Inuit have had a varied diet over the past 100 years. Traditionally, the Inuit depended on animal meat and fish for survival. The Inuit ate all parts of the animal, including the fat, bones, and blood, to ensure they had the proper vitamins and nutrients.

Vegetables could not be grown in the frozen soil. Seaweed, nuts, and berries helped fill the gap in the Inuit diet. The Inuit gathered these foods in the summer months and dried them for the winter. Animal meat was also dried, smoked, or salted to preserve it during the long winter months. An Inuit meal often included bannock, a type of bread.

Pemmican was one of the most important parts of the Inuit diet. It was made from dried meat, animal fat, and berries or nuts. The mixture was mashed together and dried or stored in containers. People took it on long journeys because it did not spoil.

Many Inuit eat Arctic char. This type of fish can be eaten raw, frozen, dried, or cooked.

RECIPE

Bannock

Ingredients

1,000 millilitres flour

2.5 millilitres salt

25 millilitres baking powder

375 millilitres water

Equipment

A large mixing bowl

Measuring cups

A baking pan

1. Mix the ingredients together in a large bowl.

2. Sprinkle flour on a flat, clean surface, and knead the dough.

3. Roll the dough into a loaf.

4. Bake for 30 minutes at 175 degrees Celsius.

5. Serve with jam or honey.

Transportation

Vehicles were among the most important tools used by the Inuit. As they hunted and followed herds, they had to sometimes travel long distances. Sleds called *komatiks* were pulled by one or more dogs. The sleds were used to carry people, supplies, and animals across land.

Transportation on water was also important for the survival of the Inuit. Kayaks were used for hunting and fishing. The Inuit used *umiaks* to transport people and goods from site to site. These boats were larger and deeper than kayaks. Both boats were made by stretching animal skins over a frame made from wood or animal bones.

Today, the Inuit still travel in umiaks when they hunt whales.

HUNTING AND SURVIVAL

Inuit weapons were used mostly for hunting. Spears, harpoons, and knives were critical to Inuit survival.

The *unaq*, a type of harpoon, was used to hunt sea mammals, such as seals and whales. The harpoon had an end piece that was connected to a rope. The hunter used the rope to pull the animal to him.

The *kakiavak* was used to catch fish in shallow water. This harpoon had three sharp prongs on it, which were used to trap and kill the fish. Another tool, called the *nitsiq*, was used to pull animals from the water. A sharp hook on the end of a long handle was used to pull animals that had been harpooned out of the water.

The Inuit used harpoons to hunt whales and seals.

Snow goggles were worn to reduce the glare from sunlight hitting the snow. The goggles could be made from ivory, leather, or wood.

Inuit Religion

The Inuit believed that all things in nature should be respected. They believed that plants, animals, people, and natural landmarks had a spirit that should be honoured. The Inuit told stories about these great spirits. These stories were used to teach each other about the proper way to treat nature and other people.

Religious leaders were called *angakkuit*. They had the power to heal the sick and speak to spirits. The spirits helped warn the angakkuit of bad weather and told them where there would be good hunting and fishing grounds. The angakkuit would then share this information with the rest of the community.

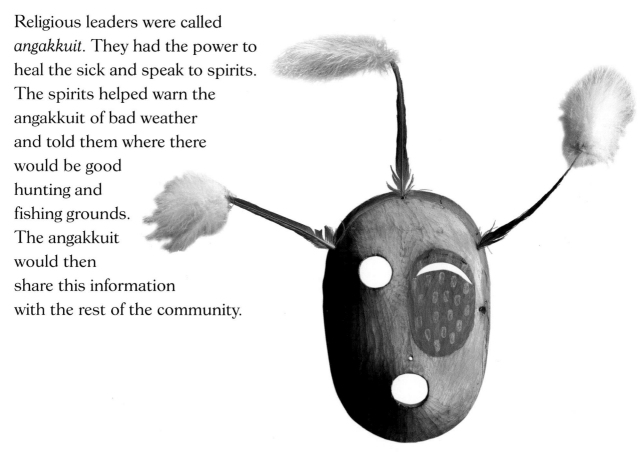

Masks were used to represent characters from the spirit world.

ANIRNIIT

When Europeans arrived in the 1800s and 1900s, they brought their **Christian** religions with them. They introduced Christian teachings to the Inuit, and many Inuit became Christian as a result. Today, many Inuit continue to practise Christianity. However, the traditional stories and music of their ancestors are still passed from generation to generation.

According to an Inuit belief called *anirniit*, all living things had a spirit, or soul. This included animals, which the Inuit depended on for survival. The Inuit believed that the soul did not disappear after a living creature was dead. It lived on and could act kindly or negatively towards the living. For this reason, the Inuit believed that it was important to honour the animals they killed and used for food, clothing, and tools. The Inuit also believed that spirits could help them.

St. Jude's Cathedral, which was shaped like an igloo, was a well-known tourist attraction in Iqaluit. It was destroyed by fire in 2005.

Inuit Celebrations

The Inuit held many celebrations and festivals throughout the year. These celebrations were a time to give thanks for good fortune and special events. People often celebrated with their families and communities.

Many Inuit festivals celebrated nature and the seasons. Spring was an important time. In the Arctic, much of the winter is spent in near or total darkness. In April, Inuit communities celebrated the Sun's return by singing and dancing. Another spring festival was the *nalukataq*, or whaling festival. This celebration was held after a whale hunt to offer thanks for its success.

Inuit celebrations typically included a large feast, dancing, music, and games. The focus of these celebrations was to enjoy and share in each other's company.

Dancing and drumming are an important part of Inuit celebrations.

When Europeans arrived, they introduced Christian celebrations to the Inuit. Today, many Inuit celebrate Christian traditions and holidays. Some of these celebrations combine Christian traditions with Inuit traditions. *Quviasukvik* is similar to the Christian Christmas celebration. It features feasting and the exchanging of gifts.

Inuit communities throughout northern Canada work to preserve their traditions by holding feasts and festivals during the year. These festivals remind people of the traditions of their ancestors. People participate in events such as dogsled or snowmobile racing, drumming, dancing, igloo building, and community feasts.

One popular game played at many Inuit festivals was the blanket toss. The game was played with a large walrus skin or sealskin. People stood in a circle around the skin and held it up like a trampoline. Each player would take turns jumping on the skin and being tossed by the people holding it. The goal of the game was to see who could be tossed the highest.

Blanket tossing is still done today, but it is now competitive. Players are scored on the positions and moves they make while being tossed, as well as the heights they reach.

The person participating in the blanket toss will sometimes throw out candy to the crowd.

Music and Dance

Music is an important part of Inuit life. Traditionally, music was performed at celebrations to give thanks for a happy event or important time of year. Drum dancing is one of the most important types of music in Inuit **culture**. In the past, large groups of people would gather to participate.

To begin the drum dance, a group of singers, usually women, would sit in a large circle and begin singing to coax a dancer into the circle's center. Before entering the circle, the dancer, usually a man, would pick up a drum and then begin dancing and drumming inside the circle. When the dancer finished performing, he would put the drum down so the next dancer could have his turn.

The Inuit have used drums in their music and celebrations for many centuries.

The drums were made from wood and animal skins. There was a small stick inside the drum for the dancer to hold while dancing. He used his other hand or a large mallet to keep the pulsing beat. Drum dances often continued for hours.

THROAT SINGING

Singing was an important part of Inuit celebrations. The songs were about people in the community, the blessings and hardships of life, and Inuit beliefs. One popular type of song was the *katajjaq*. The katajjaq was held as a competition between a minimum of two participants. Singers faced each other and sang a series of notes and sounds. Some were meant to imitate animals or birds.

The singers would work together to combine their voices to make interesting sounds. This type of singing is called throat singing. Katajjaq was competitive because it was difficult to hold the notes for a long time. The first person to disrupt the song lost the competition.

Throat singing was traditionally performed by women as entertainment while their husbands were away hunting.

Language and Storytelling

Inuit communities across the Arctic region speak different languages. In Canada, the Inuit speak Inuktitut. Inuktitut is spoken in many different **dialects**, depending on the region where a person is from. Until the arrival of Europeans, the Inuit did not have a written language. They communicated orally and through carvings and art. European **missionaries** taught the Inuit a form of writing called syllabics. This is a system of writing that uses symbols to represent letters and sounds.

The Inuit developed a strong tradition of storytelling. Inuit stories were told for fun as well as to teach important lessons. They were also used to pass down the history of the Inuit to future generations.

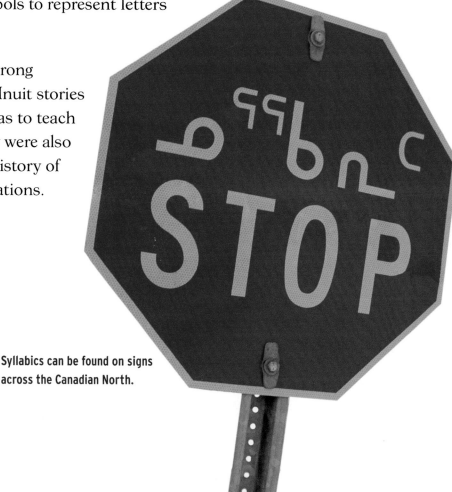

Syllabics can be found on signs across the Canadian North.

Stories were often accompanied by music, dance, and string games. In a string game, long pieces of string were tied in knots to show important parts of the story. The storyteller held the string and wove it into different patterns and shapes. Some string games were very complicated and required up to four people to participate.

String games were used to tell stories during the long winters.

NULIAJUK

Nuliajuk, also called Sedna, was one of the most powerful spirits worshipped by the Inuit. She was believed to be the mother of all sea creatures. Nuliajuk is featured in many Inuit stories. According to legend, when Nuliajuk was a young girl, she did not want to get married. As punishment, her father forced her to marry a dog. When he realized the mistake he had made, he drowned the dog. After some time, Nuliajuk married a bird that had disguised itself as a man. When she discovered the trick, she asked her father to help her escape. Nuliajuk tried to escape in a boat, but her husband caught her and turned over her boat with his large wings. As she fell into the sea, she lost her fingers. Those fingers became the many creatures that called the waters home.

Inuit Art

The Inuit are well known for their sculptures and prints. Inuit artists get inspiration from their surroundings, history, and culture.

Most Inuit sculptures are made from stone found in the Arctic region. Bones and ivory are also used. Different types of stone are used depending on the region where the people live. Soapstone and serpentine are the most commonly used. Serpentine comes in a variety of colours, including black, brown, and green. Inuit artists also use quartz and marble in their sculptures.

The style of sculpture and **finish** varies from region to region. Some Inuit sculptures have a matte, or dull, finish. Artists use this finish to highlight the natural beauty of the stone. Other artists prefer a polished, or shiny, finish. They create this effect by rubbing shoe polish or melted beeswax over their completed work of art.

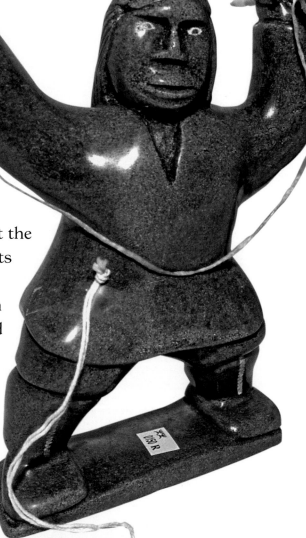

Inuit sculptures often depict people or animals.

Art prints are another form of Inuit art. Prints are made by carving a pattern or design into a piece of stone. First, ink is rolled over the stone. The stone is then pressed onto a sheet of paper or animal skin. The areas that are not carved leave an imprint on the paper. This becomes the print. Inuit art prints traditionally show scenes from daily life, stories, and the history of the Inuit.

The Inuit are known around the world for their unique carvings. Many Inuit sculptors sell their art to tourists and art galleries.

The Inuit have always used materials from their natural surroundings to create artwork. They carved rock, bones, and ivory to create tools. They also created decorative masks and rock carvings.

One mask found near the Hudson Strait in Quebec was carved from ivory. The mask, which depicts a face, is believed to be about 2,000 years old. It is called the Tyara mask, after the name of the site where it was found.

Rock carvings, called petroglyphs, have been found in the same region. They also show faces. Archaeologists are not sure if the faces represent people or spirits. The carvings were made nearly 1,000 years ago.

These carvings give clues about what life was like for the Inuit in the past. They also help **archaeologists** know where the Inuit lived and hunted thousands of years ago. Finally, they show the beginnings of a long history and tradition of beautiful artwork that continues today.

Bone Carvings

The Inuit believed that animals were **sacred**. However, in order to ensure their own survival, the Inuit had to hunt these sacred creatures. The Inuit practised many **rituals** and ceremonies to honour the animals that helped them to survive. One way they honoured them was to use all parts of the animal so that nothing went to waste.

Initially, items were carved for everyday use. Knives, combs, jewellery, and masks were carved from the bones of whales, walruses, and caribou. They were often elaborately decorated with intricate patterns and designs. Following the arrival of Europeans, the purpose of Inuit carvings began to change. The carvings were created as works of art more than decorative tools.

Still, the focus has stayed the same, with animals remaining the primary subject. Today, the animals are sometimes interpreted in abstract styles. The size of the works has a greater range, from the very small to the very large.

Family scenes, especially those featuring mothers and children, are becoming more common in Inuit art.

MODERN ARTIST

Kenojuak Ashevak

Kenojuak Ashevak was born in 1927. As a child, she moved often. Her family travelled between hunting camps on Baffin Island and northern Quebec. Kenojuak lived for part of the year in an igloo. Kenojuak and her family lived a traditional Inuit lifestyle.

Kenojuak's career as an artist began when she was very young. Living in the Arctic, she learned from an early age how to make clothing and crafts. Kenojuak used her artistic talents to experiment with other forms of art in the late 1950s.

It was at this time that Kenojuak met James Houston, a government employee. Houston encouraged Kenojuak to experiment with her art. Kenojuak began carving stone sculptures and making decorative kamiks. She became known for her sealskin **appliqué** designs.

Kenoujuak turned to drawing. She began by drawing what she knew—the people, homes, and animals of her culture. Her drawings became some of the best known of the Inuit community, and Kenojuak became one of the first Inuit women to have her designs printed. These prints are now sold all over the world.

Kenoujuak continues to create drawings, prints, and sculptures that draw upon the history and culture of her people and the importance and beauty of nature. She has been named as a Companion of the Order of Canada.

Kenojuak was the first Inuit artist to be inducted into Canada's Walk of Fame.

Studying the Past

Archaeologists use items from the past to learn about different cultures. **Artifacts** left by the Inuit and their ancestors give archaeologists clues about what life was like hundreds and thousands of years ago.

By studying Inuit sites, archaeologists believe that the ancestors of the Inuit originally crossed the Bering Strait from Siberia and settled in Alaska. On the coast, they fished and hunted whales and seals. Their homes were made from sod and wood.

Around 1,000 years ago, these ancestors moved eastward from Alaska and settled in Canada's Far North, continuing to travel and settle as far as northern Quebec. As evidence of their settlements, archaeologists have found remains of the low stone houses that some Inuit people used as shelter in the winter.

Archaeological studies in Canada's Arctic help people understand how the Inuit lived in the past.

TIMELINE

11,000 years ago

People migrate from Siberia to North America. In 1996, scientists confirm this when they discover identical tools in a city in Siberia and parts of Alaska and Canada.

4,000 years ago

A group of people move from Alaska towards northern Canada. These people are known as the pre-Dorset people. They are the earliest-known ancestors of the Inuit in Canada.

3,000 years ago

The Dorset people live in the Baffin Island area. They begin to use more advanced tools and weapons.

1,000 years ago

More people move from Alaska, leading to the eventual disappearance of the Dorset people. These people, known as the Thule, move across northern Canada and into Greenland. Over time, the Thule become the first Inuit group to use dogs for transportation and hunting. They also become the first to build igloos for shelter in the winter.

500-100 years ago

Europeans begin to explore Canada's North. Eventually, many Inuit groups are displaced as the land becomes the property of Canada and the United States.

100 years ago to the present

In the early 1900s, people begin to promote the rights of Inuit Peoples throughout the Arctic. In 1999, the Canadian government reduces the size of the Northwest Territories to create a new territory called Nunavut. People continue to champion the rights of Inuit Peoples and look for ways to preserve their long and important history.

Today, people in Nunavut celebrate the creation of the territory each July 9. This holiday is called "Nunavut Day."

Make an Inukshuk

The Inuit often travelled long distances between their winter and summer hunting grounds. They did not have maps or advanced forms of communication. To help each other travel and find plentiful hunting and fishing grounds, the Inuit built stone statues called inukshuks. Inukshuks were made from rocks piled on top of one another to form the shape of a person. They were used as landmarks to help people stay on course during their journey.

You can build your own inukshuk by following these steps.

Materials
10-12 small stones or pebbles, glue

1. Start putting the rocks together to form the shape of a person.

2. When each rock is balanced on another rock, glue the rocks together.

3. Continue balancing and gluing the rocks until the inukshuk shape is complete.

Further Reading

Discover more about the Inuit by reading their legends in *James Houston's Treasury of Inuit Legends* by James Houston (Harcourt, 2006).

Learn about the lives and works of Inuit artists in *Arctic Adventures: Tales from the Lives of Inuit Artists* by Raquel Rivera (Groundwood Books, 2007).

Websites

To learn more about the history and daily life of the Inuit, navigate to **www.collectionscanada.ca/ settlement/kids/021013-2071-e.html**.

Interact with Inuit culture by visiting the virtual museum at **www.civilization.ca/aborig /inuit3d/vmcinuit_e.html**.

View the Inuit art collection of the Canadian government at **www.ainc-inac.gc.ca/art /inuit/index2_e.html**.

GLOSSARY

INDEX

ancestors: relatives who lived a very long time ago

appliqué: the art of sewing or gluing pieces of fabric onto a larger piece of fabric for decoration

archaeologists: scientists who study objects from the past to learn about people who lived long ago

artifacts: items, such as tools, made by a human being

Christian: a person who practises a religion based on the teachings of Jesus Christ

climate: the type of weather and average temperature in a particular location

culture: the arts, beliefs, habits, and institutions characteristic of a community, people, or country

dialects: variations on a language that is spoken in a certain place

economic: having to do with the management of income, supplies, and expenses of a community

elders: the older and more influential people of a community

finish: a polished surface

heritage: the places, people, and culture of the past

migration: to move from one place to another because of the weather

missionaries: people who teach others about Christianity

rituals: systems or forms of special ceremonies

sacred: worthy of religious worship

territory: a region in Canada that has its own elected council and is administered by a commissioner appointed by the Canadian government

traditions: established beliefs, opinions, and customs